# Why *was* AMERICA *Attacked?*

# Why *was* AMERICA *Attacked?*

ANSWERS FOR A NATION AT WAR

# D. JAMES KENNEDY

BROADMAN
&HOLMAN
PUBLISHERS

NASHVILLE, TENNESSEE

Published by Broadman & Holman Publishers,
Nashville, Tennessee
Printed in the United States of America

"Two Questions for You," originally published in booklet form as *Do You Know?*, is reprinted by kind permission of Evangelism Explosion International. *Do You Know*, copyright © 1997 by Evangelism Explosion International, is available from Evangelism Explosion at 1-888-567-3543.

Scripture quotations are from the King James Version of the Bible.

# Contents

# Preface

Do you remember when you first learned on September 11 that America had been attacked? From out of a perfectly clear sky, a commercial airliner turned guided missile ripped into a World Trade Center tower. The sickening horror of the first assault only grew as many of us watched another plane slam into the second World Trade Center tower. Shortly thereafter, the Pentagon, the citadel of America's national defense, was hit in this series of senseless strikes that has left America reeling, groaning under a weight of grief, and eager to avenge the loss of more than 6,000 lives at the World Trade Center, the Pentagon, and on United Airlines Flight 93, which went down in western Pennsylvania.

Who can fully fathom the mammoth and monstrous scope of this tragedy? We mourn for the thousands who have lost husbands, wives, sons, and daughters. But as we grieve, we must also steel ourselves for war against a phantom enemy who hits and runs and may yet live among us.

Suddenly, everything is altered.

It is my hope and prayer that you will find comfort, courage, and direction as you read this brief booklet. We have included a message I delivered the first Sunday after the attacks, answers to some of the questions many are asking in the wake of this sudden tragic change in our nation, and a detailed Gospel presentation that asks the two most important questions each of us will ever answer.

I am so grateful that our President urged our nation to prayer in the immediate aftermath of the events of September 11. That is a wonderful departure from the current reign of political correctness. We will need much prayer—and repentance—before this crisis has passed.

May this booklet help you comprehend these events from a biblical perspective and aid you in your intercession for our nation. May God bless America.

# When the Towers Fall

*"And the angel of the LORD said unto her, Behold, thou art with child, and shalt bear a son, and shalt call his name Ishmael; because the Lord hath heard thy affliction. And he will be a wild man; his hand will be against every man, and every man's hand against him; and he shall dwell in the presence of all his brethren."*
—*Genesis 16:11–12*

*"And there shall be upon every high mountain, and upon every high hill, rivers and streams of waters in the day of the great slaughter, when the towers fall."*
—*Isaiah 30:25*

Before September 11, 2001, none of us had the faintest inkling of the catastrophic events that would transpire. Indeed, how true the Scripture is when it reminds us that we know not "what a day may bring forth" (Proverbs 27:1).

With millions of others across the nation, in spite of our differences—Americans all—we join together to share the grief and mourn the loss experienced by more than 6,000 families who have had one who perhaps they loved more than life itself ripped from their bosom and their grasp. Indeed, it is tragic beyond our ability to express. As we have seen the images replayed over and over again of those jets slicing into those great towers like a knife through sticks of butter, our hearts have cried out, "O Lord, let it not be! O God, let it not be!"

But how could such things happen to America? We are not at war—at least most of us didn't *believe* we were at war. I'm afraid that most have forgotten that exactly five years ago, in August of 1996, Osama bin Laden declared war on the United States. And so, unbeknownst to most of us, we, indeed, have been at war for some time and are now experiencing some of the horrors that war always brings—surely beyond our description. It has often been said by those who have experienced it that "War is Hell." Now many Americans right here at home have discovered the truthfulness of that statement.

The experts, people engaged in gathering information, have told us about what our foes are supposedly going to do and that this illusive man, Osama bin Laden, is indeed the mastermind behind this and a number of other terrorist acts. Several years ago two of our embassies in East Africa were bombed, and again the evidence pointed to bin Laden—the man who inherited a fortune and is using it to carry out his own twisted ideas of justice and righteousness. This is, indeed, tragic.

## A War on America

We have an adversary in this world bent upon our destruction and determined to do nothing less than to destroy Americans. It is a war on America conceived by bin Laden, the leader of the largest revolutionary Islamic group in the world, who has been responsible for who knows how many attacks on Americans and on Christians. What kind of man is he that all of our intelligence points to as the probable mastermind behind this?

Of course, he is descended from Ishmael, who, we are told in Scripture, "will be a wild man; his hand will be against every man, and every man's hand against him" (Genesis 16:12). It is interesting that bin Laden may have wanted to give the idea that this is the whole Islamic or Arabic world against America, but there were people in the World Trade Center from 60 other nations. This one person has succeeded in turning almost the entire civilized world against him. There were people there from Australia, and they are very angry with him—people there from many other countries. Yes, there is going to be worldwide anger when the names of all of these victims are finally known.

Now, let me make it clear that though this man is a radical follower of Islam, his views are not held by all Muslims. I am sure there are many Muslims in this country who are very grieved about what has happened and would not think of doing such a thing. There have also been Christians in past times who have killed people, but the interesting and important thing to remember is that when Christians have done this, they have done it in violation and opposition to the teachings of Jesus—not in obedience to them. That is not the case in Islam.

You are familiar, no doubt, with the "jihad," which is the declaration of a "holy war." Sudan, in the early 1990s, less than a decade ago, declared a jihad in that country. They have killed two million innocent people since then, a great many of whom were Christians. In Indonesia, a jihad has been declared against Christians in that nation. Other nations at other times have declared jihads.

Mohammed was once asked in the Hadith, which is a record of Mohammed's life and sayings second in authority to the Koran, "What is the best deed?"

He replied, "To believe in Allah and his apostle" (Mohammed was supposedly his apostle).

The questioner then asked, "What is the next (in goodness)?"

He replied, "To participate in jihad (religious fighting) in Allah's cause" (Sahih Bukhari Volume 1, Book 2, Number 25). That was their second most important commandment.

Christ was asked what is the greatest commandment.

He answered, "Thou shalt love the Lord thy God with all thy heart, and with all thy soul, and with all thy mind. This is the first and great commandment. And the second is like unto it, Thou shalt love thy neighbor as thyself" (Matthew 22:37–39).

Dear friends, if you cannot see a radical difference between those two things, you are utterly blind!

Mohammed commanded Muslims to fight against all infidels, if they do not embrace Islam, as well as against the people of the Scriptures, that is, Jews and Christians. Furthermore, the Hadith (Volume 1, page 22, as cited in

Robert Morey, *An Analysis of the Hadith*, published by
Faith Defenders, PO Box 7447, Orange, CA 92863)
speaks of conversion to Islam by compulsion. Mohammed
said, "I have been ordered to fight against the people until
they testify that none has the right to be worshiped but
Allah, that Mohammed is Allah's prophet, that they offer
prayers and give obligatory charity. If they perform all of
that, they save their lives and their property" (Sahih
Bukhari, Volume 1, Book 2, Number 24).

Mohammed warned the king of the Byzantines: "If
you become a Muslim, you will be safe" (Sahih Bukhari,
Volume 1, Book 1, Number 6). But if the king did not
convert, he and his kingdom would be destroyed and
enslaved. Mohammed further said, "Whosoever has
killed an enemy and has proof of that will possess his
spoils" (Sahih Bukhari, Volume 4, Book 53, Number
370).

Concerning Jews and Christians, Mohammed said,
"Any Jew or Christians who heard about me and did not
believe in me and what was revealed to me of the Holy
Koran and my traditions, his ultimate destination is the
(Hell) fire" (Volume 1, page li, as cited in Morey, *An
Analysis of the Hadith*). He says further that, "Allah has

cursed the Jews and the Christians because they took the graves of their prophets as places for worship" (Sahih Bukhari, Volume 2, Book 23, Number 414).

Dear friends, there is an infinite gulf between these teachings and the teaching of Jesus Christ that "thou shalt love thy neighbor as thyself."

We read in Isaiah about the great slaughter when the towers collapsed, "when the towers fall." The Bible has a number of things to say about towers. Do you remember that Jesus was talking about the 18 people who died when the tower of Siloam fell? The tower of Siloam was in Jerusalem at the pool of Siloam, and He said, "Do you suppose that those upon whom the tower of Siloam fell were worse than others? I say unto you, 'Nay, but except ye repent, ye shall all likewise perish'" (see Luke 13:4–5).

The Scriptures make it very clear that many times in the Old Testament God told His people that if they did not repent of their sins, He would bring in the foreigner, those people from far nations, and use them to chasten His own people. "If so be they will hearken, and turn every man from his evil way, that I may repent me of the evil, which I purpose to do unto them because of the evil of their doings" (Jeremiah 26:3).

According to the Scriptures, when such things as these happen, we should consider our own sins and the sins of our own nation; this is the first place we should look. I don't know about you, but this tragedy has caused me to consider, confess, and repent of my own sins. Has it done the same for you? I hope it will do so for every American. God used the Babylonians and the Assyrians and the Egyptians, and who knows what other groups, as chastening rods to punish His own people for their sins.

But "If my people, which are called by my name, shall humble themselves, and pray, and seek my face, and turn from their wicked ways; then will I hear from heaven, and will forgive their sin, and will heal their land" (2 Chronicles 7:14). We need to remember that we are called upon by God in such times as this to consider our own sins and the sins of our nation.

Dear friends, we have enough sin in this country to keep terrorists busy for the next hundred years, and we need to confess those. We need, as citizens of this nation, to confess our national sins and ask God to cleanse us and forgive us that we might be spared that which God says He has intended to do to His people. Judgment begins at the house of God, so we need to consider ourselves.

No doubt we also need to consider the evil hearts of the people who have done this. I would not in any way mitigate the horrendous evil of people that have no thought for human life and would willfully kill thousands of people out of some misguided view that they have been commanded to kill all of their enemies. I don't know about you, but I have never personally done anything I know of against a Muslim. I have prayed for them. I have sought to share the Good News of the Gospel with them, but I have never in any way tried to hurt them. But they believe that we are the great Satan, that we are evil, and that we need to be destroyed. They have the teachings of their prophet Mohammed to encourage them to do just that. This, indeed, is tragic.

America is a peaceful nation. We are not a country that is likely to start a war, but we are not a country that, once plunged into a war, is likely to not finish it. Osama bin Laden has a great many Americans angry with him. I'm afraid this man may have declared war on the wrong country. He has given every visible proof of his intention, and I cannot see how this is going to end in anything other than the complete elimination of him and his followers from the face of this earth. Osama bin Laden's brand of terrorism has numbered days, in my opinion.

## What Should Our Attitude Be?

How should Christians view this? It seems to me, as I have listened, that a number of Christians are very confused about what their attitude should be. We have people who have declared that they are, indeed, very angry with this man and that they would kill him if they could get their hands on him. Others have said, "Now, wait a minute. You are supposed to be Christians, and Christians are to love their enemies. They are supposed to turn the other cheek. How can you say those things?" That does, indeed, create something of a problem for a Christian. What should our attitude be?

Let me see if I can make something clear that I am afraid a lot of church members don't understand. Jesus Christ, in the Sermon on the Mount (Matthew 5–7) gave us a broad picture of Christian personal ethics. There have come to be two different interpretations of the Sermon on the Mount. One, which is known as the Reformed view, is a view that we and all Reformed churches hold. The other one is sometimes called the Quaker view, embraced by those who hold to those beliefs. And there is quite a difference.

We believe that the ethics taught in the Sermon on the Mount are Christian *personal* ethics. They believe that those ethics apply *to every phase* of life, whether individual, corporate, or civic—all are bound by that particular set of ethics. We believe that that is not true, and that the Quaker belief causes many people to become confused.

Are we to be angry with the perpetrators or are we to love them? Are we to attack them or are we to turn the other cheek? What *is* the Christian position? As I said, we hold to the Reformed view that says that these Sermon on the Mount principles are *personal* Christian ethics. Civil and governmental ethics are taught in Romans 13. I commend both the Sermon on the Mount and Romans 13 to your careful study. That the Sermon on the Mount does not contain corporate or civil ethics is clearly understood by anyone who would examine it carefully.

For example, if someone smites you on the right cheek, Christ said "turn to him the other also." Now if civil ethics are being talked about here, then we might imagine a scene where your wife is attacked by someone who breaks into your house, beats her up unmercifully, breaks her jaw, knocks her teeth out, and leaves her badly broken and wounded. You tackle this man; he is arrested and brought into court where I am the judge, a representative of the civil government. You tell me this horrid criminal has broken into your house and brutally beaten your wife, knocked her teeth out, broken her jaw, and that you want this man prosecuted. And I, as a judge, say, "Now, just a minute, sir. Do I not understand that you are Christians?"

"Why, yes, we are."

"Well, then, that means you are supposed to turn the other cheek, correct?" It's amazing how many Christians I've seen on TV programs who are totally baffled with a scenario such as that. Then I as the judge say, "Well, ma'am, since you claim to be a Christian, and this criminal beat you and broke your jaw, then right now turn to him the other cheek and let him take a whack or two at that." How would you feel? I think you might leap over the bench and take a few whacks at me.

That is obviously absurd! Why is it absurd? Because it is not the judge's cheek that is involved.

Or, say I'm the president of a bank. You happen to deal with my bank and you have come in to make a deposit. As you are making out the certificates, you notice a very poorly dressed man who has come off the street, and as he walks up to me, you hear him ask, "You're the president of the bank aren't you?"

I say, "Yes, I am."

And he says, "Well, I want a loan."

"Oh, you do? How much would you like?"

"Oh, $1,000. Let's make it $10,000. On the other hand, let's make it $1 million because I understand, sir, the word on the street is that you are a Christian."

"Why, yes, I am."

"Now does not Jesus say, 'From him that would borrow of thee, turn thou not away,' so I'll just take my $1 million in $1,000 bills."

"OK," and I start passing out the money. You put your deposit slip in your pocket and leave the bank.

What is wrong with my doing that? It is not very complicated. The problem is that it is not my money I'm giving away. It happens to be *yours*.

The Sermon on the Mount addresses personal Christian ethics. They are not corporate or civil or governmental ethics; you find those in Romans 13, where we read that the government does not bear the sword in vain. The sword is the sign of the power to take life; here we see the power of the state. We are to act on the principles of love and mercy. The *state* operates on the principle of justice. Therefore, the state gives justice to those who have done wrong. If one has taken a life, that one is to lose his own life in the process. That is what the purpose of the state is, but it is not your purpose to kill people. If you saw someone kill someone on the street, you are not to run after him, tackle him, pull out your knife and stab him to death. Justice, in this case, is the state's job.

So don't be confused if some talk show host tries to trip you up, and I've noticed them doing this over and over again since the attacks. It should remind us that the unbeliever in situations like this always has one purpose in mind: They want to condemn God and justify themselves. Remember that. You run into it all the time. Unbelievers want to find fault with God, find fault with Christ, find fault with His Word, find fault with you as a

Christian, and justify themselves. That is what they always try to do. Don't let them pull the wool over your eyes—especially if it is somebody else's wool.

So, then, this means that I as a Christian am not to hate. We shouldn't hate anyone; we are to love our enemies. And it also doesn't mean that the government should say, "Oh, gee, we're a Christian nation. You are forgiven. Come back anytime you can get your hands on a few more commercial jets." Of course not! I hope that the full brunt of justice falls upon those people.

The things the terrorists have done are beyond my comprehension. I cannot conceive of anybody doing to innocent people—women and children, as well as men—anything as ghastly and dastardly and as cowardly as they have done. Now they go hide out in the desert, hoping that we won't find them. *We will find them.*

## Prepare to Meet Your God

"For when they shall say, Peace and safety; then sudden destruction cometh upon them, as travail upon a woman with child; and they shall not escape" (1 Thessalonians 5:3). My friends, we know not what a day may bring forth. None of us knew what would happen on September 11, 2001, and you don't know, nor do I, what will happen tomorrow. The Bible says: Prepare to meet your God.

So I would like to ask you today: Are you prepared? If, indeed, you were on the 104th floor of one of those buildings as it began to sink and then plummet toward the earth, knowing that your last moments were now before you, do you know, do you have the assurance that you would be with God today, that you would meet Him rejoicing and not with fear and terror?

That is something only Christ can offer to the world. He says, "I am he that liveth, and was dead; and, behold, I am alive for evermore" (Revelation 1:18), and those of you that trust in Him shall live also. We can be assured that we are going to be with Him.

I talked to a man recently and asked him if he was prepared, and try as he may, he couldn't bring himself to say that he knew that were he to die next week that all would be well with his soul. Do you know that? Let me ask you this question, one familiar to many but unfamiliar no doubt to some of you. If that were to have happened to you, and instead of having a business appointment at ten o'clock that morning, you found yourself with that most important appointment of all, would you be ready?

For it is appointed unto man to stand before the almighty God at the Great Assize, the final Judgment Day, when the tomes will be opened and the destinies of men will be read out. In that glorious day, when you are confronted by God and He asks you, "What right do you have to enter into my Heaven?" what will you tell Him?

I think that such an event as we have had transpire demands that each of us consider in our own hearts and minds the ultimate question. Of all of the questions you have ever been asked in school, or wherever, none even comes close in importance. "What right do you have to enter into my Heaven?" What would you tell God?

I remember when I was just 24 years of age, a frivolous young man, as unfortunately many are today, flitting my life away on superficial things, not giving a thought to God or to Christ, and yet supposing myself to be a Christian. However, Christ had no part of my life from earliest morning until latest night—no part of my life. I never thought about Him, prayed to Him, never read His Word or sought to obey Him.

Then I was confronted with the kind of question I just mentioned to you. When my alarm clock radio came on, I heard the then-famous Presbyterian minister from Philadelphia, Dr. Donald Grey Barnhouse, a great scholar and a powerful preacher, asking loudly: "***Young man . . .***" · That will wake you up in a hurry! I didn't know what had happened; I thought somebody was in my room.

"Young man, if you were to die tonight and stand before Almighty God, and He were to say to you, 'What right do you have to enter into my Heaven,' what would you say?" I turned about four different shades of white and sat up on the edge of my bed and listened in utter astonishment to the ultimate question of life—of life and death and eternity. What *would* I say?

And I ask you this day, what would *you* say? What right do you have to enter into God's Heaven? I'd like for you to answer that question, silently, right now. "God, you should let me into Heaven because . . . ."

This was my answer. I said, "Because I have tried to live a good life. I have tried to follow the Ten Commandments, live by the Golden Rule, do the best I could." It turns out Dr. Barnhouse wasn't talking to me, but was narrating a discussion he had had with an Air

Force pilot. He told us the pilot's answer, which was, "I've tried to do the best I can and keep the Ten Commandments, follow the Golden Rule and live a good life"—virtually the same thing I said, to which I responded, "Ah, I haven't been to church in ten years, and I got it right!" If you are not laughing, you have a problem because I could not have possibly been more wrong.

## What Is the Answer?

Then he said on the radio, but seemingly to me, what he said to the pilot: "Lieutenant, if you had the audacity to say such a thing to the all-holy God who knows your every thought and deed, He would have instantly plunged you into the lake of fire." He had my attention! I listened while Dr. Barnhouse explained the glorious Gospel of Jesus Christ, and I learned for the first time in my life the most amazing thing I have ever, before or since, learned.

In all of the studies since that day long ago, I have never learned anything as important as this—a very simple statement, only three words long. I hope you will carve it on the walls of your mind: *Heaven is free! Heaven is FREE!* The Bible puts it this way: "The wages of sin is death; but the gift of God is eternal life through Jesus Christ our Lord" (Romans 6:23). The gift of God is eternal life through Jesus Christ our Lord. It's free! It's free to us, but it was paid for at infinite cost by Jesus Christ upon the Cross. He paid for it with His own life, His own blood shed for us upon that tree, and He offers it freely to us.

Have you received that gift? Do you know beyond any peradventure of a doubt that it is yours, that you have it? Should you be involved in an automobile accident, in the moment when the windshield glass collapses in front of you and the impact is felt in your body, do you know that you will be taken immediately to be with Him in Paradise? There is nothing I have learned in all of the years I spent in graduate school upon graduate school that even comes close to being as important as that. Heaven is a free gift, paid for by Christ, and offered to all of us that will place our trust in Him.

You may not have noticed, but I told you the name of my "savior." I told Dr. Barnhouse, and I told everyone here the name of my savior that morning in my bedroom when I heard that radio program. Did you notice the name of the savior I gave? I'll say it again: "I've lived a good life. I've done the best I can. I've kept the Ten Commandments, and I've followed the Golden Rule."

Well, I didn't exactly give you a noun, but I gave you a pronoun. Did you notice what it was? "I." "I." "I." "I." I had a savior whose name was "I." It was "Jim." Today I have a Savior whose name is Jesus. There is an *infinite* difference between the two.

Ah, dear friends, we need to be ready. I think that the suddenness, the unexpectedness of these events absolutely cry out for us to realize how important it is to be ready for that great appointment that is absolutely certain and yet absolutely uncertain. It is certain that we will die, but it is uncertain as to when that will be.

Are you ready to meet Him? Prepare to meet your God. We know not what a day will bring forth.

## Lessons from Disaster

The wonder of knowing the love of Jesus Christ is something that dispels all hatred and fills our hearts with the glorious love that is poured out from Him. It is wonderful to have the assurance that regardless of what tragedy may befall us, we will be with Him forever. That is the most important lesson I believe we can derive from this great disaster that has met our nation.

What was going on in those 220 floors of the two towers? It was world trade. There were hundreds of thousands of pieces of paper that contained all manner of business documents of vital importance to the 50,000 people who were working there. Employees were bending over desks and examining the various reports. Their very existence was wrapped up in those pieces of paper. One minute later those documents were confetti, flittering down from the sky, being walked upon by the dirty shoes of men, totally meaningless. Those people, alas, in many cases, had never considered the really important things in life that begin with our relationship to the God who created us.

Has that relationship been established in your life? Is Christ yours?

I am hopeful that out of this tragedy we will see a new surge of patriotism in this nation. I have seen more flags in the past week than I think I have in the last ten years, and I hope that number will grow. I am sure it will because you can't even buy them; there are long waiting lines at the stores. That is very encouraging, especially when we have been through a time in this country where many people have shown few examples of patriotism. I could not tell you how many times my wife has put the eight-foot pole and flag out in front of our house, yet when I have driven up and down our street, there was no other flag to be seen. There are flags flying on that street today, I am happy to say.

But more than a surge of patriotism, I hope that this will be the beginning of a great spiritual revival—that God may once again have His place in our land. Many people have heard the Gospel message since the attacks, but those same people would not have heard the Good News if the jet planes had not crashed into the buildings.

Now, we certainly wish that such a thing had never happened, but God is able to bring good even out of the most horrid circumstances. That is the wonderful promise we claim—out of all of this He will be glorified and the lives of millions of people will be enriched. And though more than 6,000 people lost their lives, I hope that out of this, five million people or more will come to receive life everlasting as a result and that America once more will, in truth, be one nation under God.

*Father, should there be anyone who has not yet entered into that personal relationship with Jesus Christ, who has not yet received Him as Savior and Lord, may they right now say in the intimacy of their own souls, "Lord Jesus Christ, Son of God, Savior of Men, I am a sinner, and I am sorry for my sins. Forgive me and cleanse me and make me whiter than snow. I ask You to come into my heart, to forgive me and grant me the gift of eternal life. I accept You as Lord and Savior of my heart, and right now I receive the wondrous free gift of everlasting life." In Thy most blessed name. Amen.*

# Answers from Dr. Kennedy

*In the midst of a national crisis like this, it's natural that many questions should be going through the minds of people, such as "Where was God in the midst of all of this? Why does He allow things like this to happen?" and many other questions. I'd like to offer answers to some of those questions to aid your understanding and, I pray, minister God's comfort and peace to your heart.*

## Why did God allow this to happen?

We know that the Scriptures discuss this in a number of different settings, and the answers to *all* such problems are not given in the Bible. God doesn't tell us everything we would like to know, but He does tell us those things we have to know.

"Why does God allow suffering in the world?" He has His own purposes. We do know certain things, such as the Scripture teaches that the whole world has fallen into sin and that all of us are guilty of sin and, therefore, we all are deserving of punishment. He also tells us that His own children receive chastening from Him and if we don't receive His chastening, we are not legitimate children of God. Furthermore, the Bible tells us that the suffering that comes upon various people in this world is not necessarily because of their sin—even as the man born blind. When Christ was asked, "Who did sin, this man, or his parents, that he was born blind?" Christ responded, "Neither hath this man sinned, nor his parents: but that the works of God should be made manifest in him" (John 9:2–3). Then Christ healed the man's blindness.

We also know that God has given to us a free will to do what we want. And we will be held accountable for what we do. Regardless of what happens in the military and national spheres, we know that the perpetrators of this atrocity will stand before the judgment bar of God. We also note that God is using things like this to cause us to lift our hearts unto God and to ask questions like, "What if I should meet God suddenly like that? What is my heart like? Am I ready to meet my Maker?" God may use this event to bring about a great revival in this nation.

Our hearts, of course, go out to the families of these victims. Certainly, we know that these people had nothing to do with what took place, and that they innocently were going about their daily business, when *suddenly* these planes crashed into the World Trade Center towers. We ask God for mercy upon the families—that He will comfort them and He will assuage their pain. We trust, also, that one day the culprits will be brought to justice.

## Can we feel safe if and when bin Laden or whoever is responsible is brought to justice?

We would be in error to think that Osama bin Laden is the only culprit here. There are networks of terrorists all around the world that are involved. Should he be taken out, another will fill his place. It's going to be a long drawn out effort to remove all of the people *bent* on terrorist activities. Our government has declared unequivocally that they are not going to give up; they are going to do the best they can to rid the world of such inhuman monsters who care nothing for the lives of innocent people.

## Many of us are angry. How should Christians respond?

There's no doubt that this began with much hatred in the hearts of some who hate America with a vehemence that we can hardly imagine. But we are not to respond in kind. We are told to "Love your enemies, do good to them which hate you" and not evil (Luke 6:27). Many would say, "We ought to go and pound them into oblivion!" "We ought to create another Grand Canyon somewhere in the Near East." Well, that may be the attitude of some, but it's not the attitude of a Christian.

Now, that does not mean that if we have war declared against us that we, as a nation, cannot defend ourselves. We have in the past and we no doubt will again. That is the role of the state, to execute justice. However, we, as individuals, must not hate those guilty of these wicked deeds.

When such terrible things as these have been done, it is extremely difficult to forgive. But when Christ was nailed to the Cross, His first response was, "Father, forgive them; for they know not what they do" (Luke 23:34). These people may be more aware of what they have done than the Roman soldiers were of what they had done to

Christ. I have no doubt that these people think that what they have done is just and good and righteous. They could not be more wrong. Nevertheless, that is what they believe.

We should pray that God will work in their hearts and change their lives. He did in the case of the Japanese pilot who led the raid on Pearl Harbor. This man later came to Christ, had his life transformed, and became an evangelist in Japan. The chief instrument in drawing this man to faith in Christ was a tract written by an American missionary who, during World War II, had been shot down over Japan. This American suffered great torture at the hands of his Japanese captors. But his own intense, white-hot hatred for everything Japanese was replaced with love after someone led him to Christ. After the war he returned to Japan to share Christ with the people he once hated and, in God's providence, helped bring the lead pilot at Pearl Harbor to Christ. The two men even evangelized in Japan together.

May God likewise draw some of those responsible for this act of unprecedented terror to repentance and salvation in Christ. That is the response I hope will come out of this, so Christ will get the glory.

## So, you believe that good can come out of this tragedy?

Yes. God has told us that He can turn *all* things together for good to them that love Him and who are the called according to His purpose. We know that if we truly believe in Him, we have His promise that should our life suddenly be cut off, we will be with Him in Paradise. Therefore, He can turn the greatest tragedy into the greatest good.

We also believe that at such times as this there are fantastic opportunities to *proclaim* the glad tidings of the Gospel—that many people whose hearts had been hardened are now softened and they are willing to hear, to listen, and to try to find out if "they are right with God themselves?" If they should suddenly meet their Maker, what would the result of that encounter be? So there are wonderful opportunities for all of us as Christians to share the Gospel.

## Is this attack a judgment from God?

We should be very clear that it is the terrorists who bear the responsibilities for these deeds. But we know from the Scriptures that God has often chastened His own people (in the Old Testament, the Jews) for their sins, and He has used foreigners—such as the Babylonians or the Assyrians—to come in and to *inflict* that chastening upon His own people. And so we should all consider ourselves and ask God for forgiveness for our individual sins and, as representatives of this nation, for our national sins. There is no doubt that in America we have been engaged in all kinds of immorality—every conceivable kind. We seem to be bent on plunging ourselves ever deeper and deeper into the mire of perversion and immorality. We need to repent as a nation or we can experience worse chastening from God.

## Is the U.S. military response justified?

I believe that a proper military response is essential if we are going to maintain our freedom and not make America simply a "punching bag" for anybody in the world who wants to destroy Americans. If we don't as a nation respond, we're going to face some very, very difficult days to come.

Let me say, unequivocally, that I hate war. In fact, every right-minded person hates war. War is a great evil. Only tyrants, aggressors, madmen, and the devil love war.

Thousands, millions, tens of millions of people have lost their lives in the thunderous inferno that is war.

I am definitely not a militarist, but I am not a pacifist either. The pacifist position is that no war is justified, that there is no such thing as a "just" war. Pacifists ask, as Dr. Gleason Archer has said, "How could a good God, a God of peace, condone warfare?" How could Jesus Christ, the Prince of Peace condone warfare?

And yet, as Dr. Archer says, the Bible, in referring to such wars as that of Reuben, Gad, and Manasseh against the pagan tribes of the Transjordan, states, "For there fell down many slain, because *the war was of God*" (1 Chronicles 5:22, italics added). That concept is repeated many times throughout the Old Testament.

The first just war is described in Genesis 6:8–20, where Abraham took 318 men to retrieve his nephew Lot and others taken captive by three kings who had invaded the land around the Dead Sea. Abraham quickly prevailed against the enemy and recovered all the prisoners and the goods taken.

Most people would have thought that a man like Abraham, a man noted for his piety and godliness, would certainly not be a man likely to engage in warfare. Or, if he did, that he would do it successfully. But Abraham's piety did not prevent his military exploit. In fact, it undergirded and strengthened him in the task because he trusted in God.

The Christian Church has maintained that there was and is such a thing as a "just" war, as well as an "unjust" war. In fact, down through the history of the Church, the greatest of its theologians and Reformers have held that this is true. St. Augustine, the greatest mind in the first thousand years after Paul; Thomas Aquinas, the greatest theologian of the Roman Catholic Church; Luther, Calvin, Knox, and other Reformers, down to our day, have held that there is such a thing as a "just" war. Well, what is it?

First of all, it is defensive in nature; it is for the purpose of protecting life and liberty of those who have been plundered, of those who have been attacked by offensive warfare.

Second, it is waged by a legitimate government and not by individuals. We are told over and over again in the Bible that we are not to practice personal vengeance. The Bible says, "Vengeance is mine; I will repay saith the Lord" (Romans 12:19b). Vengeance is out, but justice must be maintained—and only by the proper governmental authorities.

Furthermore, the purpose of a "just" war is to establish permanent peace and not for the purpose of personal aggrandizement. After his victory, Abraham absolutely refused to take anything from his venture in warfare. He would not take so much as a thread or a shoelace, but rather trusted in God for what he had.

There are a number of other qualities of a just war, and all of these, I believe, have been fulfilled in the case of the present conflict. This war is necessary in order to end a great evil that flies in the face of all international peace and order.

## It appears that Muslim extremists perpetrated these assaults. What does the Koran say about such acts? Are we to fear people of the Islamic faith?

The Koran teaches that followers of Allah are to oppose those of other beliefs. Here is an excerpt from the Koran that provides an insight into the attitude of strict Muslims toward those outside the mosque: "Fight against such of those to whom the Scriptures were given as believe neither in Allah nor the Last Day, who do not forbid what Allah and His apostle have forbidden, and do not embrace the true faith, until they pay tribute out of hand and are utterly subdued" (Koran, chapter 9, verse 29, in N. J. Dawood, *The Koran*, London, England: The Penguin Group, 1956, p. 323).

The Koran also teaches that those who perish for Allah will rejoice in Paradise. The 19 men who committed suicide in their terrible mission were grossly deceived into believing that their act would usher them into Paradise. The Koran states, "You must not think that those who were slain in the cause of Allah are dead. They are alive, and well provided for by their Lord; pleased with His gifts and rejoicing that those whom they left behind and who have not yet joined them have nothing to fear or to regret; rejoicing in Allah's grace and bounty Allah will not deny the faithful their reward" (Koran, chapter 3, verse 170, in Dawood, *The Koran*, p. 422).

Despite the threat posed by militant Islam, we as believers should not be afraid. They are not our enemy, but captives of our enemy, Satan. We must pray for them, share the Gospel with them, support mission enterprises into Islamic nations, and refuse to allow fear to enter our hearts. We can do this as we remember the One in whom we trust and look only to Him for our confidence and security.

## Is there a distinction to be made between moderate, peace-loving Muslims and those who carried out this cruel attack?

We should keep in mind that there are many Muslims (many of them live in this country) that are as appalled as we are at these events and who have had nothing to do with them. We should not hold all of them indiscriminately guilty for what has happened. They are no guiltier than are you or I. We ought to be very careful to put the blame only on those that deserve it.

## Islamic militants believe that suicide missions give them a one-way ticket to Heaven—to Paradise. What will actually happen to them?

These suicide bombers are taught that they will be taken immediately into Paradise where seven lovely virgins will await them. The fact is that they will discover that the same kind of inferno they have created in these buildings will be awaiting them in Hell.

# Will America ever be the same after this horrible attack?

Will America ever be the same again? I hope not. Now I'm sure that's the last thing you expected me to say. Of course, in some ways, I hope it will be the same in the sense that we will not experience such terrible calamities again.

On the other hand, I hope the nation will be different in that the hearts of the people of this country will once more be drawn to God, and that there will be a *spiritual* revival, and that we will *turn* from our wicked ways and seek the face of God, and that there will be a great moral improvement in this country. That also could be a result of these terrible things. It is my prayer that this heinous act may be used of God to bring about a great spiritual revival.

# What practical suggestions can you give for people who want to help in the aftermath of the attack?

We all want to continue to pray for this nation. We want to give to help rebuild it. We want to provide the needed blood for those who are injured and in hospitals now. We had a large blood drive here at Coral Ridge

Presbyterian Church to try to help provide for the needs of those who have been wounded. We hope that you will give and pray, and that God in the midst of all of this will fulfill His promise to turn *all* things to our good.

## How can we best pray for our President?

At this time we ought to be faithfully and regularly praying for our President and all of those in authority over us in government. We should ask God to give them wisdom and show them what to do. We should also pray that God would cause these criminals to be exposed and to be captured, in order to bring an end to such mindless terror as this and that the people of America might once again walk the streets of this country without fear.

## What can parents tell their anxious children who have already seen this tragedy—and will see this hundreds of times in the weeks ahead on TV?

As a young boy, I will never forget those words spoken in 1941 by then-President Franklin Delano Roosevelt: "This is a day that will live in infamy." I will never forget those words, just as children today, who have seen the startling video of commercial airplanes flying into office towers, have an image seared into their mind that they will never forget.

The events of September 11, amplified by the endless replays of the attacks in New York City, have brought fear and anxiety into the hearts of many children. I believe parents should shield their children from those powerful images, which are very frightening to little ones. They need to offer their children the opportunity to talk about what they may have seen, to pray with them, and to comfort them from God's Word.

This terrible time provides an opportunity to introduce your child to the spiritual wealth of the Psalms, which offer abundant comfort for anxious hearts. Psalms 23, 27, 46, and 91 are just a few examples of the comfort to be found in His Word.

## Did this take God by surprise? Did it occur outside His control?

Some people have asked, "Was God taken by surprise?" The answer to that is obviously "no" because God is omniscient and has known *all* things from eternity. Nothing happens that God does not at least allow.

He allows even evil men to exercise the will He has given them, and unfortunately they too often use that for evil deeds. But God is sovereign over all and is working all things together for the good of those that love Him and believe in Him.

# Two Questions for You

*What if you had been on one of the hijacked flights, or working at your desk at the World Trade Center when the planes attacked? Do you know what your eternal destination would be had you died September 11? You can know for certain! Find out how below.*

1. *Do you know for sure that you are going to be with God in Heaven?*

2. *If God were to ask you, "Why should I let you into My Heaven?" what would you say?*

You don't know? Then here is the THE BEST NEWS YOU COULD EVER HEAR! The few minutes it will take you to read these pages may be the most important time you will ever spend!

Did you know that the Bible tells HOW YOU CAN KNOW FOR SURE that you have eternal life and will go to be with God in Heaven?

*"These things I have written unto you . . . ; that ye may know that ye have eternal life" (1 John 5:13).*

HERE'S HOW: The Bible says there are 5 THINGS you need to know about eternal life:

## 1. HEAVEN

**ETERNAL LIFE IS A FREE GIFT!**
The Bible says,

> *". . . the GIFT of God is eternal life*
> *through Jesus Christ our Lord"*
> *(Romans 6:23, emphasis added).*

And because HEAVEN IS A GIFT, like any other genuine gift . . . IT IS NOT EARNED OR DESERVED.

No amount of personal effort, good works, or religious deeds can earn a place in Heaven for you.

*"For by grace are ye saved through faith; and that not of yourselves: it is the GIFT of God: NOT OF*

*WORKS, lest any man should boast"*
*(Ephesians 2:8–9).*

WHY is it that no one can earn his way to Heaven? Because . . .

## 2. MAN

**MAN IS A SINNER**

*"For all have sinned, and come short of the*
*glory of God" (Romans 3:23).*

Sin is transgressing God's law and includes such things as lying, lust, cheating, deceit, evil thoughts, immoral behavior, and more.

AND BECAUSE OF THIS MAN CANNOT SAVE HIMSELF.

If you wanted to save yourself by good deeds, do you know how good you would have to be?

*"Be ye therefore perfect, even as your Father which*
*is in heaven is perfect" (Matthew 5:48).*

With such a high standard, no one can save himself.

HOWEVER, IN SPITE OF OUR SIN . . .

## 3. GOD IS MERCIFUL

And therefore doesn't want to punish us.

This is because ". . . God is love" (1 John 4:8). And He says, ". . . I have loved thee with an everlasting love" (Jeremiah 31:3).

But the same Bible which tells us that God loves us, also tells us that . . .

### GOD IS JUST

And therefore must punish sin. He says
*"(I) will by no means clear the guilty . . ."*
*(Exodus 34:7).*
*". . . the soul that sinneth, it shall die"*
*(Ezekiel 18:4).*

WE HAVE A PROBLEM. God loves us and doesn't want to punish us, but He is just and must punish sin.

God solved this problem for us in the Person of . . .

## 4. JESUS CHRIST

### WHO IS HE?

The Bible tells us clearly that He is the infinite GOD-MAN.

*"In the beginning was the Word (Jesus) . . . and the Word (Jesus) was God. And the Word (Jesus) was made flesh, and dwelt among us" (John 1:1, 14).*

Jesus Christ came to earth and lived a sinless life, but while on earth . . .

### WHAT DID HE DO?

He died on the Cross to pay the penalty for our sins and rose from the grave to purchase a place for us in Heaven.

*"All we like sheep have gone astray; we have turned every one to his own way; and the* LORD *hath laid on Him (Jesus) the iniquity (sin) of us all" (Isaiah 53:6).*

Jesus Christ bore our sin in His body on the Cross and now offers you eternal life (Heaven) as a free gift.

This gift is received by faith.

## 5. FAITH IS THE KEY THAT OPENS THE DOOR TO HEAVEN.

Many people mistake two things for saving faith:

1. Saving faith is not mere INTELLECTUAL ASSENT, like believing certain historical facts. The Bible says that the devil believes there is one God, so believing that there is one God is not saving faith.

2. Saving faith is not mere TEMPORAL FAITH, that is, trusting God for temporary crises such as financial, family, or physical needs. Now these are good, and you should trust Christ for these, but they are not saving faith!

### SAVING FAITH

Is trusting in Jesus Christ alone for eternal life. It means resting upon CHRIST ALONE and what HE HAS DONE, rather than in what you or I have done to get us into Heaven.

> " . . . *Believe (trust) on the Lord Jesus Christ, and thou shalt be saved . . ."* (Acts 16:31).

You have just read the GREATEST STORY ever told about the GREATEST OFFER ever made by the GREATEST PERSON who ever lived—JESUS CHRIST.

The question that God is asking you now is . . .

### WOULD YOU LIKE TO RECEIVE THE GIFT OF ETERNAL LIFE?

Because this is such an important matter . . .
LET'S CLARIFY JUST WHAT IT INVOLVES.
It means that you need to:

- **TRANSFER YOUR TRUST**
  from what you have been doing to what Christ has done for you on His Cross.

- **ACCEPT CHRIST AS SAVIOR**
  Open the "door" to your heart and invite
  Him in.

*He says: "Behold, I stand at the door, and knock: if
any man hear my voice, and open the door,
I will come in to him . . ." (Revelation 3:20).*

- **RECEIVE JESUS CHRIST AS LORD**
  Give Him the "driver's seat" and "controls" of
  your life, not the "back seat."

- **REPENT**
  Be willing to TURN from anything that is not
  pleasing to Him. He will reveal His will to you
  as you grow in your relationship with Him.

Now, if this is what you really want . . .

## YOU CAN GO TO GOD IN PRAYER . . .

. . . right where you are. You can receive His gift of eternal life through Jesus Christ right now.

> *"For with the heart man believeth unto*
> *righteousness; and with the mouth confession is*
> *made unto salvation. . . . For whosoever shall call*
> *upon the name of the Lord shall be saved"*
> *(Romans 10:10, 13).*

If you want to receive the gift of eternal life through Jesus Christ, then call on Him, asking Him for this gift right now.

### HERE'S A SUGGESTED PRAYER:

*"Lord Jesus Christ, I know I am a sinner and do not deserve eternal life. But, I believe You died and rose from the grave to purchase a place in Heaven for me. Lord Jesus, come into my life; take control of my life; forgive my sins and save me. I repent of my sins and now place my trust in You for my salvation. I accept the free gift of eternal life."*

If this prayer is the sincere desire of your heart, look at what Jesus promises to those who believe in Him:

*"Verily, verily, I say unto you, he that believeth on Me hath everlasting life" (John 6:47).*

### WELCOME TO GOD'S FAMILY!

- If you have truly repented (forsaken, turned away) from your sins
- Placed your trust in Jesus Christ's sacrificial death
- And received the gift of eternal life
- You are now a child of God! Forever!

Welcome to the Family of God!

*"But as many as received him, to them gave he power to become the sons of God, even to them that believe on his name" (John 1:12).*

# TODAY IS YOUR SPIRITUAL BIRTHDAY!

A day you will always want to remember!

The Bible speaks of those who receive eternal life in these words:

> *"Which were born, not of blood, nor of the will of the flesh, nor of the will of man, but of God"*
> *(John 1:13).*

When you were physically born, the day of your birth was attested by a birth certificate. And so today, to help you recall what God has done in your life on this important day, we invite you to sign and keep the following . . .

# *Spiritual Birth Certificate*

*"For whosoever shall call upon the name of the Lord shall be saved" (Romans 10:13).*

Knowing that I have sinned, and I need the Lord Jesus Christ as my Savior, I now turn from my sins and trust Him for my eternal life. I ask Jesus Christ to forgive me, and to deliver me from sin's power and give me eternal life.

I now give Jesus Christ control of my life. From this time forward, as He gives me strength, I will seek to trust Him and obey Him in all areas of my life.

Signature_____

Date_____

**WHAT'S NEXT?**

Just as a newborn baby grows physically, in a similar way you can grow spiritually by taking the following steps:

✔ READ THE BIBLE

Starting with the Gospel of John, read a chapter each day.

"As newborn babes, desire the sincere milk of the
Word (of God), that ye may grow thereby"
(1 Peter 2:2).

✔ PRAYER

Spend time each day talking with God.

"Be careful for nothing; but in everything by prayer
and supplication with thanksgiving let your requests
be made known unto God" (Philippians 4:6).

✔ WORSHIP

Regularly attend a church that honors Jesus Christ and teaches you the Bible.

"I was glad when they said unto me, Let us go into
the house of the LORD" (Psalm 122:1).

*"GOD is a Spirit: and they that worship him must worship him in spirit and truth"* (John 4:24).

✔ FELLOWSHIP

with Christians who will help you grow in faith.
*"That which we have seen and heard declare we unto you, that ye also may have fellowship with us: and truly our fellowship is with the Father, and with his Son Jesus Christ"* (1 John 1:3).

✔ WITNESS

Tell others what Jesus Christ means to you.
*"But ye shall receive power, after that the Holy Ghost is come upon you: and ye shall be witnesses unto Me"* (Acts 1:8b).

If you have appreciated the GOOD NEWS you have just read, please let us know. We want to rejoice in what God has done in your life and help you grow spiritually. Please call or write to Coral Ridge Ministries to let us know!

> Coral Ridge Ministries
> P.O. Box 40
> Fort Lauderdale, FL 33302
> 1-800-229-9673
> www.coralridge.org

The Gospel presentation above is provided as a gift from Evangelism Explosion International, the lay evangelism training outreach founded by Dr. D. James Kennedy.

This Gospel presentation, titled *Do You Know?*, is available in booklet form from Evangelism Explosion. To request *Do You Know?*, please call Evangelism Explosion at 1-888-567-3543.

ISBN: 0-8054-1829-6   Price: $9.99

**With one billion members and a fiercely aggressive attitude**, Muslims pose a serious challenge to expanding Christianity and world peace everywhere. With a detailed firsthand knowledge of Muslim life, Dr. George Braswell digs beneath the religion's seemingly harmless surface to reveal a rich, proud, and powerful force in world affairs. *What You Need to Know about Islam and Muslims* provides both a complete introduction and a comprehensive reference tool on Muslims–where they started; how they're positioned in today's social, political, and religious arenas; and where they're heading in the twenty-first century.

George W. Braswell Jr. (B.D., Yale; Ph.D., University of North Carolina at Chapel Hill) is Distinguished Professor of Missions and World Religion and serves as director of the D.Min. program at Southeastern Baptist Theological Seminary. Braswell lived in Iran for seven years and is the author of several books, including *Islam: Its Prophet, Peoples, Politics, and Power*.